What Every Principal Would Like to Say . . .

. . . and What to Say Next Time

What grows never grows old.

—Noah benShea

What Every Principal Would Like to Say . . .

. . . and What to Say Next Time

Quotations for Leading,
Learning, and Living

CORWIN PRESS, INC.
A Sage Publications Company
Thousand Oaks, California

For information:

Corwin Press, Inc.
A Sage Publications Company
2455 Teller Road
Thousand Oaks, California 91320
E-mail: order@corwinpress.com

Sage Publications Ltd.
6 Bonhill Street
London EC2A 4PU
United Kingdom

Sage Publications India Pvt. Ltd.
M-32 Market
Greater Kailash I
New Delhi 110 048 India

Printed in the United States of America

Library of Congress Cataloging-in-Publication Data

Main entry under title:
    What every principal would like to say . . . and what to say next time:
Quotations for leading, learning, and living / [edited] by Noah benShea.
        p.   cm.
    ISBN 0-7619-7605-1 (cloth: alk. paper)
    ISBN 0-7619-7606-X (pbk.: alk.paper)
    1. School principals—Quotations.   I. benShea, Noah.
LB2831.9 .W53 2000
371.2′012′02—dc21   99-050417

This book is printed on acid-free paper.

00   01   02   03   04   05   06   7   6   5   4   3   2   1

Editorial Assistant: Kylee Liegl
Production Editor: Diana E. Axelsen
Editorial Assistant: Cindy Bear
Typesetter/Designer: Lynn Miyata
Cover Designer: Oscar Desierto

CONTENTS

PREFACE

*W*hether you're the principal of a school, the principal figure in your company, the principal figure in your home, or, as you have finally realized, the principal figure in your own life, this book is for you. Here are ideas that will help you manage daily life intelligently and compassionately and make tomorrow more manageable.

This is more than a book of quotes. These are thoughts that are selected and framed so that you may see old problems in a new light, paint a different picture for others, and not paint yourself into a corner.

From time to time, all of us are asked to give a speech or make a few remarks. On a more regular basis, what almost all of us need is to take ourselves aside for a little talk. So, next time you're called upon by others or want to place a call to yourself, take this book with you.

The venerable actress Ruth Gordon liked to remind us that "the best impromptu speeches are the ones written well in advance." Unfortunately life doesn't always give us advance notice. Here is timeless advice in advance. It is advice that you can give others and remind yourself. Put it next to your bed, next to you in the car, on your desk, in your briefcase. It is an ally for leading, learning, and living. Wherever you're going, this book will make you wiser when you get there.

May you go from strength to strength and be a source of strength to others.

—*Noah benShea*
Santa Barbara, California

ACKNOWLEDGMENTS

I wish to thank the following members of my research team for their invaluable help in making this book possible:

Ms. Jordan Arin benShea
Mr. Adam Joseph benShea
Ms. Holly A. Williams

A giant is anyone who remembers we are all sitting on someone else's shoulders.

—*Anonymous*

ABOUT THE AUTHOR

*N*oah benShea is a poet, philosopher, scholar, and international best-selling author who was, by the age of 23, an Assistant Dean of Students at ULCA and, by 30, a consulting fellow to the Center for the Study of Democratic Institutions in Santa Barbara, California. His first book, a collection of poetry titled *Don't Call It Anything,* received the Schull Award from the Southern California Poetry Society. He has lectured at numerous universities, as well as the Library of Congress, and his work has been included in publications of Oxford University and the World Bible Society in Jerusalem.

Noah benShea's books on Jacob the Baker are translated around the world and embraced as timeless fables. His insightful perspective on life, *Noah's Window,* is carried globally via the Internet and enjoyed by countless readers through the *New York Times* Newspaper Regional Network. His essays were nominated for a Pulitzer Prize in journalism in 1997, and in 1999 he was nominated for the Grawemeyer Award for Ideas Improving World. His most recent book, *Jacob's Ladder: Wisdom for the Heart's Ascent,* is a look at life, love, and fathering. In addition to his reflective life, Mr. benShea was a founding partner and later chairman of a national manufacturing company, and he continues to serve as an advisor to North American business and community leaders. Born in Toronto, he lives in Santa Barbara, California.

This book is dedicated to the
selfless multitude of principals who sacrifice
a great deal but seldom their principles.

*He is never alone that is
accompanied with noble thoughts.*

—Beaumont and Fletcher (1647)

1

ADMINISTRATORS, PRINCIPALS, AND SCHOOL LEADERS

---

*L*eaders
are dealers
in hope.

—*Napoleon*

If you want to manage somebody, manage yourself.
Do that well and you'll be ready to stop managing.
And start leading.

—Anonymous

❧

A true leader isn't one who rules over
but one who lifts up.

—Noah benShea

❧

I've never known any human being, high or humble,
who ever regretted, when nearing life's end,
having done kindly deeds. But I have known
more than one millionaire who became haunted
by the realization that they had led selfish lives.

—B. C. Forbes

❧

Setting an example is not the main means
of influencing another, it is the only way.

—Albert Einstein

❧

Do something . . . lead, follow,
or get out of the way.

—General George S. Patton, Jr.

*Do not seek to follow in the footsteps of the men of old;
seek what they sought.*

—Basho

*All that is necessary for the triumph of evil
is for good men to do nothing.*

—Edmund Burke

*It is always easier to dismiss a man than it is to train him.
No great leader ever built a reputation on firing people.
Many have built a reputation on developing them.*

—Unknown

*Leaders must be close enough to relate to others,
but far enough ahead to motivate them.*

—John Maxwell

Leadership is action, not position.

—Donald H. McGannon

*Leadership is the capacity to
translate vision into reality.*

—Warren G. Bennis

I not only use all the brains I have, but all I can borrow.

—Woodrow Wilson

*To be a leader, you have to make people want to follow you,
and nobody wants to follow someone who
doesn't know where he is going.*

—Joe Namath

He who has a why to live for can bear almost any how.

—Nietzsche

*You do not lead by hitting people over the head—
that's assault, not leadership.*

—Dwight D. Eisenhower

*A good leader is not the person who does things right,
but the person who finds the right things to do.*

—Anthony T. Dadovano

*A true leader always keeps
an element of surprise up his sleeve,
which others cannot grasp
but which keeps his public excited and breathless.*

—Charles de Gaulle

Do not follow where the path may lead.
Go instead where there is no path
and leave a trail.

—Anonymous

❧

Good leaders develop through a never-ending process
of self-study, education, training, and experience.

—Manual on military leadership

❧

If you would win a man to your cause,
first convince him that you are his true friend.
Next, probe to discover what he wants to accomplish.

—Abraham Lincoln

❧

In order to be a leader a man must have followers.
And to have followers, a man must have their confidence.
Hence, the supreme quality for a leader
is unquestionably integrity.
Without it, no real success is possible,
no matter whether it is on a section gang,
a football field, in an army, or in an office.
If a man's associates find him guilty of being phony,
if they find that he lacks forthright integrity, he will fail.
His teachings and actions must square with each other.
The first great need, therefore,
is integrity and high purpose.

—Dwight D. Eisenhower

*In order to make a fire burn, you fan the live coals.
In order to keep your organization fired up,
it's imperative that you find and motivate the leaders
or potential leaders in your organization regardless
of how far down the line they might be.*

—Dexter Yager

❧

*It is better to have one person working with you
than three working for you.*

—Unknown

❧

*Nearly all men can stand adversity, but
if you want to test a man's character, give him power.*

—Abraham Lincoln

❧

*We forfeit three-fourths of ourselves
in order to be like other people.*

—Arthur Schopenhauer

❧

*No man will make a great leader who wants to do it
all himself or to get all the credit for doing it.*

—Andrew Carnegie

❧

*Our chief want in life is somebody who
shall make us what we can be.*

—Ralph Waldo Emerson

*R*eal leaders are ordinary people
with extraordinary determination.

—*Unknown*

*T*he first method for estimating the intelligence of a ruler
is to look at the men he has around him.

—*Niccolo Machiavelli*

*T*he first step to leadership is servanthood.

—*John Maxwell*

*T*he key to successful leadership today
is influence, not authority.

—*Kenneth Blanchard*

*T*he speed of the leader determines the rate of the pack.

—*Unknown*

*T*he very essence of leadership is that you have a vision.
It's got to be a vision you can articulate clearly and forcefully
on every occasion. You can't blow an uncertain trumpet.

—*Theodore Hesburgh*

*T*rust is the emotional glue that binds
followers and leaders together.

—*Warren Bennis and Bert Nanus*

*You can judge a leader by the size of problems he tackles—
people nearly always pick a problem their own size, and ignore
or leave to others the bigger or smaller ones.*

—Anthony Jay

You can't build a reputation on what you are going to do.

—Henry Ford

*To know how to do a job is the accomplishment of labor;
To be available to tell others is the accomplishment of the teacher;
To inspire others to do better work is the accomplishment
of management; To be able to do all three is the
accomplishment of true leaders.*

—Guy Ferguson

All management begins with self-management.

—Noah benShea

*When you bring up kids, you have to teach things over and
over and over again. As a leader, you must counsel again
and again and again. The biggest part of this business is the
relationship, not the money. Teach that over and over and over.*

—Dexter Yager

*You gain strength, experience and confidence by every expe-
rience where you really stop to look fear in the face. . . .
You must do the thing you cannot do.*

—Eleanor Roosevelt

The man who has no problems is out of the game.

—Elbert Hubbard

❧

It is the heart that makes a man rich.
He is rich according to what he is, not according to what he has.

—Henry Ward Beecher

❧

Men are rich only as they give.
He who gives great service gets great return.

—Elbert Hubbard

❧

In the middle of every difficulty lies opportunity.

—Albert Einstein

❧

The big question is whether you are going to
be able to say a hearty yes to your adventure.

—Joseph Campbell

❧

Effort only fully releases its reward
after a person refuses to quit.

—Napoleon Hill

Character cannot be developed in ease and quiet. Only through experiences of trial and suffering can the soul be strengthened, vision cleared, ambition inspired and success achieved.

—Helen Keller

❦

There are men and women who make the world better just by being the kind of people they are. They have the gift of kindness or courage or loyalty or integrity. It really matters very little whether they are behind the wheel of a truck or running a business or bringing up a family. They teach the truth by living it.

—James A. Garfield

❦

Never doubt that a small group of thoughtful, committed people can change the world; indeed, it's the only thing that ever has.

—Margaret Mead

❦

Life is a symphony. The question is how we conduct ourselves and the part we play with others.

—Noah benShea

❦

A real leader faces the music, even when he doesn't like the tune.

—Anonymous

"Management" means, in the last analysis, the substitution of thought for brawn and muscle, of knowledge for folklore and superstition, and of cooperation for force.

　　　　　　　　　　　　　　　　—Peter F. Drucker

Power corrupts, and absolute power corrupts absolutely.

　　　　　　　　　　　　　　　　—Lord Acton

He who controls the past commands the future. He who commands the future conquers the past.

　　　　　　　　　　　　　　　　—George Orwell

The power of man has grown in every sphere, except over himself.

　　　　　　　　　　　　　　　　—Winston Churchill

To command is to serve, nothing more and nothing less.

　　　　　　　　　　　　　　　　—Andre Malraux

I am certainly not one of those who need to be prodded. In fact, if anything, I am the prod.

　　　　　　　　　　　　　　　　—Winston Churchill

In simplest terms, a leader is one who knows where he wants to go, and gets up, and goes.

　　　　　　　　　　　　　　　　—John Erskine

*You cannot escape the responsibility
of tomorrow by evading it today.*
—Abraham Lincoln

❧

*Competing pressures tempt one to believe that an issue deferred
is a problem avoided; more often it is a crisis invented.*
—Henry Kissinger

❧

*Few things can help an individual more than to place
responsibility on him, and to let him know that you trust him.*
—Booker T. Washington

❧

*A good manager is a man who isn't worried about his own
career but rather the careers of those who work for him.
My advice: Don't worry about yourself. Take care of those who
work for you and you'll float to greatness on their achievements.*
—H. S. M. Burns

❧

*We are now in the third stage of the industrial revolution.
The first involved machines which extended human muscle;
the second used machines to extend the human nervous system
(radio, television, telephones); the third is now utilizing machines
which extend the human mind—computers. About half of all
service workers (43 percent of the labor force by 2000) will be
involved in collecting, analyzing, synthesizing, structuring,
storing, or retrieving information. . . . By 1995, 80 percent
of all management will be "knowledge workers."*
—Owen Davies

The productivity of work is not the responsibility of the worker but of the manager.

—Peter F. Drucker

The Trojans lost the war because they fell for a really dumb trick: hey, there's a gigantic wooden horse outside and all the Greeks have left. Let's bring it inside! Not a formula for long-term survival. Now if they had formed a task force to study the Trojan Horse and report back to a committee, everyone wouldn't have been massacred. Who says middle management is useless?

—Adam C. Engst

Remember, Custer had a plan.

—Noah benShea

A computer will not make a good manager out of a bad manager. It makes a good manager better faster and a bad manager worse faster.

—Edward Esber

I've been promoted to middle management. I never thought I'd sink so low.

—Tim Gould

You don't manage people; you manage things. You lead people.

—Admiral Grace Hooper

The greatest manager has a knack for making ballplayers think they are better than they think they are.

—Reggie Jackson

❧

Man is the principal syllable in Management.

—C. T. McKenzie

❧

Good managers have a bias for action.

—Thomas J. Peters

❧

Surround yourself with the best people you can find, delegate authority, and don't interfere.

—Ronald Reagan

❧

I would rather have a first-class manager running a second-rate business than a second-rate manager running a first-rate business.

—Jack E. Reichert

❧

Management must speak with one voice. When it doesn't, management itself becomes a peripheral opponent to the team's mission.

—Pat Riley

*Remember that when an employee enters your office,
they are in a strange land.*

—Erwin H. Schell

❧

*Management's job is to see the company not as it is . . .
but as it can become.*

—John W. Teets

❧

*A good manager doesn't try to eliminate conflict;
he tries to keep it from wasting the energies of his people.
If you're the boss and your people fight you openly
when they think that you are wrong—
that's healthy.*

—Robert Townsend

❧

*An overburdened, overstretched executive
is the best executive, because he or she doesn't have the
time to meddle, to deal in trivia, to bother people.*

—Jack Welch

2

ALTERNATIVE AND ACCELERATED SCHOOLS

I'm not a teacher, but an awakener.

—Robert Frost

Wisdom is where we have the wisdom to find it.
—Noah benShea

❧

We learn by doing real things.
—George H. Wood

❧

Scientific observation, then, has established that education is not what the teacher gives; education is a natural process spontaneously carried out by the human individual, and is acquired not by listening to words but by experiments upon the environment.
—Maria Montessori

❧

A morning-glory at my window satisfies me more than the metaphysics of books.
—Walt Whitman

❧

There are two lasting bequests we can give our children: one is roots. The other is wings.
—Hodding Carter, Jr.

❧

Imagination is more important than knowledge. Knowledge is limited. Imagination encircles the world.
—Albert Einstein

Don't smother each other. No one can grow in the shade.
—Leo Buscaglia

We must use time creatively, and forever realize that the time is always ripe to do right.
—Nelson Mandela

No bird soars too high if he soars with his own wings.
—William Blake

Empowering education educates students to fight for a quality of life in which all human beings benefit.
—Henry Giroux

There is, I think, no point in the philosophy of progressive education which is sounder than its emphasis upon the importance of the participation of the learner in the formation of the purposes which direct his activities in the learning process, just as there is no defect in traditional education greater than its failure to secure the active cooperation of the pupil in construction of the purposes involved in his studying.
—John Dewey

The good school is that one in which in studying I also get the pleasure of playing.
—Paulo Freire

Liberation is a praxis: the action and reflection of men upon their world in order to transform it.

—John Dewey

❧

The first step in promoting action outside the classroom is to transform education inside the classroom.

—Elsa Auerbach and Nina Wallerstein

❧

It is surprising how naturally students respond to being presented with choices—in any subject.

—Herbert Kohl

❧

Education can serve as the core of a lifelong journey towards wholeness, rather than merely an accumulation of facts, figures, or skills.

—Steven Glazer

❧

If we recovered a sense of the sacred, we could recover our capacity for wonder and surprise, essential qualitites in education.

—Parker J. Palmer

❧

Education is then understood to be like a mirror that allows us to glimpse and recognize our face: our true nature, our original purity. The practices of education, the various steps we take, are simply the application of different tools, techniques, and studies that help us to reach this ultimate goal.

—The Dzogchen Ponlop Rinpoche

*There are two ways of spreading light—to be the candle
or the mirror that reflects it.*

—Edith Wharton

∾

*Students—just as they are encouraged to think abstractly—
should be encouraged to see, smell, hear, touch, and taste.*

—Steven Glazer

∾

*Through education we can explain to our brothers, sisters,
and especially the young children that there is a secret treasure
we all have—whether educated or uneducated, rich or poor,
this race or that race, of this culture or that culture:
we are human beings.*

—His Holiness the Dalai Lama

∾

*Respect the child. Be not too much his parent.
Trespass not on his solitude.*

—Ralph Waldo Emerson

∾

*You don't get harmony
when everybody sings the same note.*

—Doug Floyd

Each second we live is a new and unique moment of the universe, a moment that will never be again . . . and what do we teach our children? We teach them that two and two make four, and that Paris is the capital of France. When will we also teach them what they are? We should say to each of them: Do you know what you are? You are a marvel. You are unique. In all the years that have passed, there has never been another child like you. Your legs, your arms, your clever fingers, the way you move. You may become a Shakespeare, a Michaelangelo, a Beethoven. You have the capacity for anything. You are a marvel!

—*Pablo Casals*

Wisdom begins in wonder.

—*Socrates*

The greatest good you can do for another is not just share your riches, but reveal to them their own.

—*Benjamin Disraeli*

Spirit is the real and eternal; matter is the unreal and temporal.

—*Mary Baker Eddy*

A closed mind is a dying mind.

—*Edna Ferber*

3

ASSESSMENT AND TESTING

Failure is success if we learn from it.

—Malcolm Forbes

*L*ife tests all of us. Pay attention. Take notes.

—Noah benShea

~

*I*t is child's play deciding what should be done
as compared with getting it done.

—Alan Brooke

~

*T*o choose, it is first necessary to know.

—Herman Finer

~

*I*n decision-making one should not commit himself irrevocably
to a course of action until he absolutely has to do so.

—Richard M. Nixon

~

*S*uccess can be a lot of fish or the smell of a lot of fish.

—Noah benShea

~

*E*verything depends upon circumstances:
you must sail according to the wind.

—Piconnerie de la Bugeaud

~

I am the very slave of circumstance.

—Lord Byron

Circumstances should never alter principles.

—Oscar Wilde

❧

To each circumstance its own law.

—Napoleon

❧

Growth is the only evidence of life.

—John Henry Newman

❧

The test of a first-rate intelligence is the ability
to hold two opposed ideas in the mind at the same time,
and still retain the ability to function.

—Esquire Magazine, February 1936

❧

Success is not always sprouted in success.
Failure can be a fertilizer.

—Noah benShea

❧

Experience is a hard teacher because
she gives the test first, the lesson after.

—Vernon Law

❧

You cannot create experience, you undergo it.

—Albert Camus

*The knowledge of the world is only
to be acquired in the world, and not in the closet.*

—Lord Chesterfield

❧

*The toughest thing about success is
that you've got to keep on being successful.*

—Irving Berlin

❧

Too much success can ruin you as surely as too much failure.

—Marlon Brando

❧

To win without risk is to triumph without glory.

—Corneille

❧

*There are some things we do simply
because the doing is a success.*

—Nikki Giovanni

❧

It is almost as easy to be enervated by triumph as by defeat.

—Max Lerner

❧

Success is its own burden.

—Noah benShea

A man who never made a mistake never made anything.

—Paul Muni

❧

Is there anything in life so disenchanting as attainment?

—Robert Louis Stevenson

❧

A successful life has less to do with what car you drive than what is driving you.

—Noah benShea

❧

Success means we go to sleep at night knowing that our talents and abilities were used in a way that served others.

—Marianne Williamson

❧

The tragedy of life is not that man loses but that he almost wins.

—Heywood Broun

❧

There is no failure except in no longer trying.

—Elbert Hubbard

❧

He that lies on the ground cannot fall.

—Yiddish proverb

To persevere, trusting in what hopes he has,
is courage in a man. The coward despairs.

—*Euripides*

⟨∾⟩

The soul's success requires us
to question what we consider a success.

—*Noah benShea*

⟨∾⟩

No one can make you feel inferior
without your consent.

—*Eleanor Roosevelt*

⟨∾⟩

Let the end try the man.

—*Shakespeare*

4

AT-RISK STUDENTS

*W*here there is great love
there are always miracles.

—Willa Cather

We're all at risk of being less than we might be.
The biggest risk in life is when we won't risk living.

—Noah benShea

∽

No pessimist ever discovered the secrets of the stars, or sailed
to an uncharted land, or opened a new heaven to the human spirit.

—Helen Keller

∽

Bless a thing and it will bless you. Curse it and it will
curse you. . . . If you bless a situation, it has no power to hurt
you, and even if it is troublesome for a time, it will gradually
fade out, if you sincerely bless it.

—Emmet Fox

∽

Do not weep; do not wax indignant. Understand.

—Baruch Spinoza

∽

Concern should drive us into action and not into a depression.

—Karen Horney

∽

The responsibility to make choices and
to institute change is the child's.

—Virginia M. Axline

The greatest evil that can befall man is that he should come to think ill of himself.

—Goethe

❧

Forgiveness is the final form of love.

—Reinhold Niebuhr

❧

Failure is delay but not defeat. It is a temporary detour, not a dead-end street.

—William Arthur Ward

❧

As Aristotle taught, people do not naturally or spontaneously grow up to be morally excellent or practically wise. They become so, if at all, only as the result of a lifelong personal and community effort.

—Jon Moline

❧

When we do the best we can, we never know what miracle is wrought in our life, or in the life of another.

—Helen Keller

❧

I have come to a frightening conclusion that I am the decisive element in the classroom. . . . As a teacher, I possess tremendous power to make a child's life miserable or joyous. I can be a tool of torture or an instrument of inspiration. I can humiliate or humor, hurt or heal. In all situations, it is my response that decides whether a crisis will be escalated or de-escalated, and a child humanized or dehumanized.

—Haim Ginott

Rules imposed by external constraint remain external to the child's spirit. Rules due to mutual respect and cooperation take root inside the child's mind.

—Jean Piaget

༄

While positive reinforcement should be tied specifically to real efforts and accomplishments, no matter how the child performs, it is always useful to convey messages of confident expectations. Children benefit from feelings of hope, not despair.

—Jerome Bruns

༄

The world is run by C students.

—Anonymous

༄

Treat people as if they were what they ought to be and you help them become what they are capable of being.

—Goethe

༄

In later life, as in earlier, only a few persons influence the formation of our character; the multitude pass us by like a distant army. One friend, one teacher, one beloved, one club, one dining table, one work table are the means by which one's nation and the spirit of orientation affect the individual.

—Jean Paul Richter

Only from the alliance of the one, working with and through the other, are great things born.

—Antoine de Saint-Exupery

❧

Our patience will achieve more than our force.

—Edmund Burke

❧

Love them, especially when they least deserve to be loved.

—Kate Samperi

5

CHARACTER EDUCATION

*Understand yourself
and you will
understand everything.*

—Shunryu Suzuki

No matter what we plant in our garden,
character is the gardener.

—Noah benShea

A person's character is their destiny.

—Heraclitus

If there is anything we wish to change in the child,
we should first examine it and see whether it is not something
that could better be changed in ourselves.

—Carl Jung

What grows never grows old.

—Noah benShea

The work of the individual still remains the spark
that moves mankind forward.

—Igor Sikorsky

A man cannot be comfortable without his own approval.

—Mark Twain

*Integrity simply means a willingness
not to violate an identity.*

—Erich Fromm

❧

No man is free who is not master of himself.

—Epictetus

❧

*A man who has never gone to school may steal from a
freight car, but if he has a university education
he may steal the whole railroad.*

—Franklin D. Roosevelt

❧

*What lies behind us and what lies before us are small matters
compared to what lies within us.*

—Ralph Waldo Emerson

❧

*What you see in others has more to do with who you are
than who other people are.*

—Epictetus

❧

*Dignity does not consist in possessing honors,
but in deserving them.*

—Aristotle

*Everybody thinks of changing humanity
and nobody thinks of changing himself.*

—Leo Tolstoy

What does not bend, breaks.

—Noah benShea

*The great danger for most of us
is not that our aim is too high and we miss it,
but that it is too low and we reach it.*

—Michelangelo

*We were deliberately designed to learn by trial and error.
We're brought up, unfortunately, to think that nobody should
make mistakes. Most children are de-geniused by the
fear of their parents—that they might make a mistake.*

—Buckminster Fuller

*The curious paradox is that when I accept myself
just as I am, then I can change.*

—Carl Rogers

*Society is a masked ball, where every one hides
his real character, and reveals it in hiding.*

—Ralph Waldo Emerson

Life is to be felt, not figured out.

—Thomas Hardy

We only become what we are by the radical and deep-seated refusal of that which others have made of us.

—Jean-Paul Sartre

I have an everyday religion that works for me. Love yourself first, and everything else falls into line.

—Lucille Ball

Man partly is and wholly hopes to be.

—Robert Browning

What we need are more people who specialize in the impossible.

—Theodore Roosevelt

My religion is very simple—my religion is kindness.

—Dalai Lama

Intelligence without character is a dangerous thing.
—Gloria Steinem

✑

*By constant self-discipline and self-control
you can develop greatness of character.*
—Grenville Kleiser

✑

Put more trust in nobility of character than in an oath.
—Solon

✑

Honesty is the first chapter in the book of wisdom.
—Thomas Jefferson

✑

*Within our educational institutions,
it is important that we develop more emphasis, more training,
and more exercises for the development of compassion.*
—The Dzogchen Ponlop Rinpoche

✑

*Strength isn't the absence of weakness
but how we wrestle with our weaknesses.*
—Noah benShea

✑

*Character cannot be developed in ease and quiet. Only through
experience of trial and suffering can the soul be strengthened,
ambition inspired, and success achieved.*
—Helen Keller

6

COMMUNICATION AND CONFLICT RESOLUTION

*Conflict is inevitable,
but combat is optional.*

—Max Lucado

*Understanding is living in a house
where every room has a point of view.*

—Noah benShea

❧

*Only a brave person is willing to honestly admit, and
fearlessly to face, what a sincere and logical mind discovers.*

—Rodan of Alexandria

❧

*The most important thing in communication
is to hear what isn't being said.*

—Peter Drucker

❧

What isn't said between people is also heard.

—Noah benShea

❧

*For every problem, there is one solution
which is simple, neat, and wrong.*

—H. L. Mencken

❧

*When I come upon anything—in logic or in any other
hard subject—that entirely puzzles me, I find it a capital plan
to talk it over, aloud, even when I am all alone.
One can explain things so clearly to one's self.*

—Lewis Carroll

We have two ears to hear both sides.

—Noah benShea

❧

*I have yet to see any problem, however complicated,
which, when you looked at it in the right way,
did not become still more complicated.*

—Paul Anderson

❧

Use soft words and hard arguments.

—English proverb

❧

*Feelings of worth can flourish only in an atmosphere where
individual differences are appreciated, mistakes are tolerated,
communication is open, and rules are flexible—the kind of
atmosphere that is found in a nurturing family.*

—Virginia Satir

❧

Reason explains the darkness but is not a light.

—Noah benShea

❧

Silence is argument carried out by other means.

—Ernesto Che Guevara

❧

*Never get in a shouting match with a damn fool.
Someone may walk up and not know which one is the fool.*

—Dr. Donald E. Walker

Argument is the worst sort of conversation.
—Jonathan Swift

❧

For good or ill, your conversation is your advertisement.
Every time you open your mouth
you let men look into your mind.
—Bruce Burton

❧

Never hold discussions with the monkey
when the organ grinder is in the room.
—Sir Winston Churchill

❧

Anger is a signal, and one worth listening to.
—Harriet Lerner

❧

Make sure you have finished speaking
before your audience has finished listening.
—Dorothy Sarnoff

❧

Listening is a magnetic and strange thing, a creative force.
The friends who listen to us are the ones we move toward.
When we are listened to, it creates us,
makes us unfold and expand.
—Karl Menninger

❧

When people are deaf, I am dumb.
—Joseph Joubert

In thinking, keep to the simple. In conflict, be fair and
generous. In governing, don't try to control.

—*Tao Te Ching*

∾

Fortunately psychoanalysis is not the only way to resolve
inner conflicts. Life itself remains a very effective therapist.

—*Karen Horney*

∾

The harder the conflict, the more glorious the triumph.
What we obtain too cheap, we esteem too lightly; it is dearness
only that gives everything its value. I love the man that can smile
in trouble, that can gather strength from distress and grow brave
by reflection. 'Tis the business of little minds to shrink; but he
whose heart is firm, and whose conscience approves his conduct,
will pursue his principles unto death.

—*Thomas Paine*

∾

In the frank expression of conflicting opinions
lies the greatest promise of wisdom in governmental action.

—*Louis D. Brandeis*

∾

I happen to feel that the degree of a person's intelligence
is directly reflected by the number of conflicting attitudes
she can bring to bear on the same topic.

—*Lisa Alther*

*Washing one's hands of the conflict
between the powerful and the powerless means
to side with the powerful, not to be neutral.*

—Paulo Freire

❧

*If the person you are talking to
doesn't appear to be listening, be patient.
It may simply be that he has
a small piece of fluff in his ear.*

—Pooh's Little Instruction Book,
inspired by A. A. Milne

❧

*Nonviolence is the answer
to the crucial political and moral questions of our time;
the need for mankind to overcome oppression and
violence without resorting to oppression and violence.
Mankind must evolve from all human conflict
a method which rejects revenge, aggression, and retaliation.
The foundation of such a method is love.*

—Martin Luther King, Jr.

7

COMMUNITY RELATIONS AND PARENTAL INVOLVEMENT

*B*ehold, how good
and pleasant it is for people
to dwell together in unity.

—Book of Psalms

No child is an island. Each is a part of the main.
                                        —Noah benShea

✎

The joys of parents are secret, and so are their griefs and fears.
                                        —Francis Bacon

✎

*The best brought-up children are those who have seen their
parents as they are. Hypocrisy is not the parents' first duty.*
                                        —George Bernard Shaw

✎

*Don't limit a child to your own learning,
for he was born in another time.*
                                        —Rabbinical proverb

✎

*I must study politics and war, that my sons may have the
liberty to study mathematics and philosophy, geography, natural
history, and naval architecture, navigation, commerce, and agri-
culture, in order to give their children a right to study painting,
poetry, music, architecture, statuary, tapestry and porcelain.*
                                        —John Adams

✎

Parents are the bones on which children cut their teeth.
                                        —Peter Ustinov

*Y*our children need your presence more than your presents.

—Rev. Jesse L. Jackson

*I*t is the malady of our age that the young are so busy teaching us that they have no time left to learn.

—Eric Hoffer

*I*n order to influence a child, one must be careful not to be that child's parent or grandparent.

—Don Marquis

*P*erhaps no place in any community is so totally democratic as the town library. The only entrance requirement is interest.

—Claudia "Lady Bird" Johnson

A community is like a ship; everyone ought to be prepared to take the helm.

—Henrik Ibsen

*I*n every community, there is work to be done. In every nation, there are wounds to heal. In every heart, there is the power to do it.

—Marianne Williamson

A school system without parents at its foundation is just like a bucket with a hole in it.

—Rev. Jesse L. Jackson

With such a parent there is such a child.

—Japanese proverb

Perhaps parents would enjoy their children more if they stopped to realize that the film of childhood can never be run through for a second showing.

—Evelyn Nown

Children are likely to live up to what you believe of them.

—Claudia "Lady Bird" Johnson

The most important thing that parents can teach their children is how to get along without them.

—Frank A. Clark

Any kid who has two parents who are interested in him and has a house full of books isn't poor.

—Sam Levenson

Respect the child. Be not too much his parent. Trespass not on his solitude.

—Ralph Waldo Emerson

Where parents do too much for their children, the children will not do much for themselves.

—Elbert Hubbard

*Nothing exerts a stronger psychic effect
upon the environment, and especially upon children,
than the [unlived] life [of] the parents.*

—Carl Jung

*To educate a person in mind and not in morals
is to educate a menace to society.*

—Theodore Roosevelt

Who is ignorant? Those who do not educate their children.

—The Talmud

*Most American children suffer too much mother
and too little father.*

—Gloria Steinem

*The family is the association established by nature
for the supply of man's everyday wants.*

—Aristotle

*Children should be led into the right paths,
not by severity, but by persuasion.*

—Terence

*A man can seldom—very, very, seldom—fight a
winning fight against his training: the odds are too heavy.*

—Mark Twain

Parents are patterns.

—*American proverb*

❧

Children help parents find feelings
they never knew were lost.

—*Noah benShea*

COUNSELING

*We are all wise
for other people.*

—Emerson

We are all captains of our own ship, but no captain sets sail without a navigator.

—Noah benShea

✦

Friendly counsel cuts off many foes.

—Shakespeare

✦

You will always find some Eskimos ready to instruct the Congolese how to cope with heat waves.

—Stanislaw Lec

✦

Do people conform to the instructions of us old ones? Each thinks he must know best about himself and thus many are lost entirely.

—Goethe

✦

No grand idea was ever born in a conference, but a lot of foolish ideas have died there.

—F. Scott Fitzgerald

✦

As a bamboo conduit makes a round jet of water, so taking counsel together rounds men to one mind.

—Malay proverb

*Where no counsel is, the people fall:
but in the multitude of counselors there is safety.*

—English proverb

❧

Just as the twig is bent, the tree's inclined.

—Alexander Pope

❧

*He who would learn to fly one day must first learn to stand
and walk and run and climb and dance; one cannot fly into flying.*

—Friedrich Nietzsche

❧

No man ever listened himself out of a job.

—Calvin Coolidge

❧

*Advice is like snow; the softer it falls, the longer it dwells
upon, and the deeper it sinks into, the mind.*

—Samuel Taylor Coleridge

❧

*It has seemed to be more necessary to have regard to the
weight of words rather than to their number.*

—Cicero

❧

*Fewer things are harder to put up with
than the annoyance of a good example.*

—Mark Twain

Don't fight forces; use them.

—Buckminster Fuller

∾

What is important is to keep learning, to enjoy challenge, and to tolerate ambiguity. In the end there are no certain answers.

—Matina S. Horner

∾

So I say: Don't hold back. Don't be shy. Step forward in every way you can to plan boldly, to speak clearly, to offer the leadership which the world needs.

—Claudia "Lady Bird" Johnson

∾

In giving advice I advise you, be short.

—Horace

∾

Children are like wet cement. Whatever falls on them makes an impression.

—Haim Ginott

∾

We set standards for drugs, because bad drugs cross state lines. Well, badly educated children cross state lines, too.

—Admiral Hyman G. Rickover

∾

Fears are educated into us and can, if we wish, be educated out.

—Karl A. Menninger, M.D.

I have never let my schooling interfere with my education.

—Mark Twain

T here are two ways of spreading light: to be the candle or
the mirror that reflects it.

—Edith Wharton

A master can tell you what he expects of you.
A teacher, though, awakens your own expectations.

—Patricia Neal with
Richard DeNeut

A great teacher never strives to explain his vision—
he simply invites you to stand beside him and see for yourself.

—Rev. R. Inman

I f you would thoroughly know anything, teach it to others.

—Tryon Edwards

T o teach is to learn twice.

—Joseph Joubert

A n idea can turn to dust or magic,
depending on the talent that rubs against it.

—William Bernbach

The greatest aid to adult education is children.
—Charlie T. Jones and Bob Philips

Every adult needs a child to teach; it's the way adults learn.
—Frank A. Clark

A teacher affects eternity.
—Henry B. Adams

*A teacher should have maximal authority
and minimal power.*
—Thomas Szasz

*The true teacher defends his pupils
against his own personal influence.*
—A. B. Alcott

*Consult: To seek another's approval
of a course already decided on.*
—Ambrose Bierce

*Education does not mean teaching people
to know what they do not know; it means
teaching them to behave as they do not behave.*
—John Ruskin

When a man's education is finished, he is finished.

—E. A. Filene

❧

Ask counsel of him who governs himself well.

—Leonardo da Vinci

❧

Though men will often give you advice freely,
you will often be cheated if you take it.

—George Dennison Prentice

❧

No enemy is worse than bad advice.

—Sophocles

❧

Those who build to everyone's advice
will have a crooked house.

—Danish proverb

DISCIPLINE

Before we can conquer the world we must be able to conquer ourselves.

—Alexander the Great

What we stop doing is sometimes
the most important thing we can do.
— Noah benShea

❧

The difference between perseverance and obstinacy
is that one often comes from a strong will,
and the other from a strong won't.
— Henry Ward Beecher

❧

The greatest intellectual capacities are only found
in connection with a vehement and passionate will.
— Arthur Schopenhauer

❧

Self-respect is the fruit of discipline; the sense of dignity
grows with the ability to say no to oneself.
— Abraham Joshua Heschel

❧

Morale is self-esteem in action.
— Avery Weisman

❧

Establishing goals is all right if you don't let them
deprive you of your interesting detours.
— Doug Larson

I've always wanted to be somebody,
but I see now I should have been more specific.

—Lily Tomlin

❧

Self-discipline is when your conscience tells you
to do something and you don't talk back.

—W. K. Hope

❧

A man cannot be comfortable without his own approval.

—Mark Twain

❧

The hardest thing to learn in life
is which bridge to cross and which to burn.

—Laurence J. Peter

❧

The best discipline, maybe the only discipline
that really works, is self-discipline.

—Walter Kiechel III

❧

You can find on the outside
only what you possess on the inside.

—Adolfo Montiel Ballesteros

Discipline is the refining fire by which talent becomes ability.

—Roy L. Smith

❧

It's a funny thing about life; if you refuse to accept anything but the best, you very often get it.

—W. Somerset Maugham

❧

One half of life is luck; the other half is discipline— and that's the important half, for without discipline you wouldn't know what to do with your luck.

—Carl Zuckmayer

❧

Like all weak men he laid an exaggerated stress on not changing one's mind.

—W. Somerset Maugham

❧

There are those who would misteach us that to stick in a rut is consistency—and a virtue, and that to climb out of the rut is inconsistency—and a vice.

—Mark Twain

❧

Resolve must be firmer, spirit the bolder, courage the greater, as our strength grows less.

—Anonymous

He who conquers others is strong.
He who conquers himself is mighty.

—Lao-Tzu

He that would govern others,
first should be master of himself.

—Philip Massinger

He is most powerful who has power over himself.

—Seneca

It's not how much you push along the way,
it's what you have in you to finish.

—Michael Jordan

Democracy is the art of disciplining oneself
so that one need not be disciplined by others.

—Georges Clemenceau

Ours is a world where people don't know what they want and
are willing to go through hell to get it.

—Don Marquis

*E*xecute every act of thy life as though it were thy last.

—Marcus Aurelius

*D*o not consider painful what is good for you.

—Euripides

*I*f men live decently, it is because
discipline saves their very lives for them.

—Sophocles

I am, indeed, a king, because I know how to rule myself.

—Pietro Aretino

*W*hat lies in our power to do, it lies in our power not to do.

—Aristotle

*D*iscipline is not a simple device for securing
superficial peace in the classroom; it is the morality
of the classroom as a small society.

—Emile Durkheim

*S*elf command is the main elegance.

—Ralph Waldo Emerson

10

DIVERSITY

As long as you keep a person down, some part of you has to be down there to hold him down, so it means you cannot soar as you otherwise might.

—Marian Anderson

Doing something differently can make all the difference.

—Noah benShea

Species without diversity do not survive.

—Biological truth

Segregation was wrong when it was forced by white people, and I believe it is still wrong when it is requested by black people.

—Coretta Scott King

Men are taught to apologize for their weaknesses, women for their strengths.

—Lois Wyse

If we cannot now end our differences, at least we can help make the world safe for diversity.

—President John F. Kennedy

You can't have all chiefs; you gotta have Indians too.

—American proverb

*To have doubted one's own first principles
is the mark of a civilized man.*

—Oliver Wendell Holmes, Jr.

❧

Assimilation is evaporation.

—Israel Zangwill

❧

*Use what talent you possess: the woods would be very silent
if no birds sang except those that sang best.*

—Henry VanDyke

❧

*Speak not against anyone whose burden
you have not weighed yourself.*

—Marion Bradley

❧

Wipe your finger before you point to my spots.

—Dr. Donald E. Walker

❧

*An age is called Dark, not because the light fails to shine,
but because people refuse to see it.*

—James A. Michener

❧

Every subculture has its own pathology.

—Marcel Proust

I would rather live in a world where my life is a mystery than live in a world so small that my mind could comprehend it.

—Harry Emerson Fosdick

America is a religious nation, but only because it is religiously tolerant and lets every citizen pray, or not pray, in his own way.

—Editorial in the New York Times

America is a place where Jewish merchants sell Zen love beads to agnostics for Christmas.

—John Burton Brimer

America did not invent human rights. In a very real sense, it is the other way around. Human rights invented America.

—Jimmy Carter

America is not like a blanket—one piece of unbroken cloth. America is more like a quilt—many patches, many pieces, many colors, many sizes, all woven together by a common thread.

—Rev. Jesse L. Jackson

The test of courage comes when you are in the minority. The test of tolerance comes when we are in the majority.

—Ralph W. Stockman

Democracy does not guarantee equality,
only equality of opportunity.

—Irving Kristol

❧

Democracy is a small hard core of common agreement,
surrounded by a rich variety of individual differences.

—James B. Conant

❧

Sometimes a majority simply means that
all fools are on the same side.

—Claude McDonald

❧

There's no place you can go any longer and escape
the global problems, so one's thinking must become global.

—Theodore Roszak

❧

I look to a time when brotherhood needs no publicity,
to a time when an award for brotherhood would be as
ridiculous as an award for getting up each morning.

—Daniel D. Mich

❧

The human race has improved everything except the human race.

—Adlai E. Stevenson

*In America everybody is of the opinion that he has
no social superiors, since all men are created equal,
but he does not admit that he has no social inferiors.*
—Bertrand Russell

*I have a dream that my four little children will one day live
in a nation where they will not be judged by the color of their skin
but by the content of their character.*
—Martin Luther King, Jr.

*It is a wise man who said that there is no greater inequality
than the equal treatment of unequals.*
—Felix Frankfurter

*A racially integrated community is a chronological term
timed from the entrance of the first black family
to the exit of the last white family.*
—Saul Alinsky

*No one has been barred on account of his race
from fighting or dying for America—there are no "white" or
"colored" signs on the foxholes or graveyards of battle.*
—John F. Kennedy

*America has the best-dressed poverty
the world has ever known.*
—Michael Harrington

Society is a more level surface than we imagine.
Wise men or absolute fools are hard to be met with,
as there are few giants or dwarfs.

—William Hazlitt

❧

There are no elements so diverse that
they cannot be joined in the heart of a man.

—Jean Giraudoux

❧

Men are born equal but they are also born different.

—Erich Fromm

❧

When two do the same thing,
it is not the same thing after all.

—Publilius Syrus

11

EARLY CHILDHOOD EDUCATION

If the first button of one's coat is wrongly buttoned, all the rest will be crooked.

—Giordano Bruno

A twig is a tree in training.

—Noah benShea

The great man is he who does not lose his child-heart.

—Mencius

Every child is an artist. The problem is how to remain an artist once he grows up.

—Pablo Picasso

If you treat men the way they are, you never improve them. If you treat them the way you want them to be, you do.

—Goethe

Character building begins in our infancy, and continues until death.

—Eleanor Roosevelt

Grow up, and that is a terribly hard thing to do. It is much easier to skip it and go from one childhood to another.

—F. Scott Fitzgerald

To see things in the seed, that is genius.

—Lao-Tzu

*E*very child born into the world is a new thought of God,
an ever-fresh and radiant possibility.

—Kate Douglas Wiggin

❧

*M*y degree was a kind of inoculation. I got just enough
education to make me immune from it for the rest of my life.

—Alan Bennett

❧

I learn the way monkeys learn—watching its parents.

—Charles, Prince of Wales

❧

*T*he prolonged education indispensable to the progress of
society is not natural to mankind.

—Winston Churchill

❧

*W*e are faced with the paradox that education has become
one of the chief obstacles to intelligence and freedom of thought.

—Bertrand Russell

❧

*E*ducation is what survives when
what has been learnt has been forgotten.

—B. F. Skinner

*I always tell students that it is what you learn
after you know it all that counts.*

—Harry S. Truman

❧

*Childhood is measured out by sound and smells
And sights before the dark of reason grows.*

—John Betjeman

❧

*There is always one moment in childhood
when the door opens and lets in the future.*

—Graham Greene

❧

*There is a window in our forehead which is open when we are
very young, and we spend our days at the open window staring
at the world. Around the age or four or five the window is shut
and the longing we feel for childhood is a longing for a time
when we sat staring out that window.*

—Theodore Sturgeon

❧

*The business of being a child interests a child not at all.
Children very rarely play at being other children.*

—David Holloway

❧

*My mother loved children—she would have
given anything if I had been one.*

—Groucho Marx

*W*hen I was young I looked like Al Capone
but lacked his compassion.

—Oscar Levant

*C*hildhood is the kingdom where no one dies.

—Edna St. Vincent Millay

A child's spirit is like a child, you can never catch it
by running after it; you must stand still, and, for love,
it will soon itself come back.

—Arthur Miller

*N*othing would induce me to go over my childhood days again.
I thought I was happy because my mother said I was.

—Rev. H. R. L. Sheppard

*T*here are no illegitimate children, only illegitimate parents.

—J. Yankwich

*K*nowledge which is acquired under compulsion
has no hold on the mind. Therefore do not use compulsion,
but let early education be rather a sort of amusement; this will
better enable you to find out the natural bent of the child.

—Plato

The real object of education is to leave a man in the condition
of continually asking questions.

—Bishop Creighton

Ruth's grandchildren are at that fashionable school in
Dorset, and can already change wheels, top batteries and milk
cows. They are going to learn to read next year you say.
At ten and twelve? Isn't that a little soon?

—Rose Macaulay

All men who have turned out worth anything
have had a chief hand in their own education.

—Sir Walter Scott

Cauliflower is nothing but cabbage with a college education.

—Mark Twain

As the twig is bent, the tree's inclined.

—Alexander Pope

12

EXCEPTIONAL STUDENTS

There is nothing noble about being superior to some other man. The nobility is in being superior to your previous self.

—Hindu proverb

Some of us are exceptional. Without exception all of us matter.
—Noah benShea

❧

Everyone has talent. What is rare is the courage to follow that talent to the dark place where it leads.
—Erica Mann Jong

❧

We are what we repeatedly do.
Excellence, then, is not an act, but a habit.
—Aristotle

❧

Real knowledge is to know the extent of one's ignorance.
—Confucius

❧

The brighter you are, the more you have to learn.
—Don Herold

❧

Success is that old ABC: ability, breaks, and courage.
—Charles Luckman

❧

No man can discover his own talents.
—Brendan Francis

If there is anything a man can do well, I say let him do it.
Give him a chance.

—*Abraham Lincoln*

∽

It requires wisdom to understand wisdom:
the music is nothing if the audience is deaf.

—*Walter Lippman*

∽

Nothing great was ever achieved without enthusiasm.

—*Ralph Waldo Emerson*

∽

The price of greatness is responsibility.

—*Winston Churchill*

∽

The rung of a ladder was never meant to rest upon,
but only to hold a man's foot long enough
to enable him to put the other somewhat higher.

—*Thomas Henry Huxley*

∽

Little is more exceptional than
the ability to love without exception.

—*Noah benShea*

*What we need are more people
who specialize in the impossible.*

—Theodore Roethke

❧

If heaven made him, earth can find some use for him.

—Chinese proverb

❧

*It is not because things are difficult that we do not dare;
it is because we do not dare that they are difficult.*

—Seneca

❧

*The great thing in this world is not so much where we stand,
but what direction we are moving.*

—Oliver Wendell Holmes

❧

*What you see in others has more to do
with who you are than who other people are.*

—Epictetus

❧

*Dignity does not consist in possessing honors,
but in deserving them.*

—Aristotle

Most of the shadows of this life are caused
by our standing in our own sunshine.

—Ralph Waldo Emerson

He who breathes deepest lives most.

—Elizabeth Barrett Browning

This is what knowledge really is: it is finding out something
for oneself with pain, with joy, with exultancy, with labor, and
with all the little ticking, breathing moments of our lives, until it
is ours which is rooted in the structure of our lives.

—Thomas Wolfe

Let him that would move the world first move himself.

—Socrates

He does not seem to me to be a free man
who does not sometimes do nothing.

—Cicero

Just one great idea can
completely revolutionize your life.

—Earl Nightingale

Wonder, rather than doubt, is the root of our knowledge.
—Abraham Heschel

❧

As we acquire knowledge, things do not become more comprehensible, but more mysterious.
—Albert Schweitzer

❧

There is no saint without a past, no sinner without a future.
—Ancient Persian Mass

❧

He who wants a rose must respect the thorn.
—Persian proverb

❧

All the wonders you seek are within yourself.
—Sir Thomas Brown

❧

Few is the number who think with their own minds and feel with their own hearts.
—Albert Einstein

❧

Wisdom is knowing what to do next. Virtue is doing it.
—David Starr Jordan

I find even bad people good, if I am good enough.

—Lao-Tzu

✍

When a true genius appears in the world you may know him by this sign, that the dunces are all in confederacy against him.

—Jonathan Swift

✍

After the game, the king and pawn go into the same box.

—Italian proverb

✍

Some are born to sweet delight.

—William Blake

13

FUND-RAISING AND SCHOOL FINANCE

If a person gets his attitude toward money straight, it will help straighten out almost every other area in his life.

—Billy Graham

To light a candle you must first purchase the candle.

—Noah benShea

The importance of money flows from it being a link between the present and the future.

—John Maynard Keynes

It's good to have money and the things that money can buy, but it's good, too, to check up once in a while and make sure you haven't lost the things that money can't buy.

—George Horace Latimer

Get to know two things about a man: how he earns his money and how he spends it. You will then have the clue to his character. You will have a searchlight that shows up the inmost recesses of his soul. You know all you need to know about his standards, his motives, his driving desires, his real religion.

—Robert J. McCracken

Money will come to you when you are doing the right thing.

—Michael Phillips

A man wakes up on the Sabbath and discovers a pot of gold under his bed. The man goes to reach for it and it moves away from him. The man heads off to prayer services and the money follows him.

—Yiddish proverb

*Competition brings out the best in products
and the worst in people.*

—David Sarnoff

❧

Money does not change men, it only unmasks them.

—Mme. Riccoboni

❧

*I know at last what distinguishes man from animals:
financial worries.*

—Romain Rolland

❧

*If your outgo exceeds your income,
then your upkeep will be your downfall.*

—Bill Earle

❧

Money doesn't talk, it swears.

—Bob Dylan

❧

When money talks, nobody notices what grammar it uses.

—Anonymous

❧

*Money isn't everything . . .
but it ranks right up there with oxygen.*

—Rita Davenport

Charity sees the need, not the cause.

—German proverb

❧

A bone to the dog is not charity. Charity is the bone shared with the dog, when you are just as hungry as the dog.

—Jack London

❧

Capital can do nothing without brains to direct it.

—J. Ogden Armour

❧

Money is a terrible master but an excellent servant.

—P. T. Barnum

❧

The only thing money gives you is the freedom of not worrying about money.

—Johnny Carson

❧

There's no such thing as a free lunch.

—Milton Friedman

❧

The buck stops with the guy who signs the checks.

—Rupert Murdoch

*Money is the most egalitarian force in society.
It confers power on whoever holds it.*

—Roger Starr

❧

*A bank is a place that will lend you money
if you can prove that you don't need it.*

—Bob Hope

❧

Lack of money is the root of all evil.

—George Bernard Shaw

❧

*Save a little money each month and at the end of the year
you'll be surprised at how little you have.*

—Ernest Haskins

❧

*Money it turned out, was exactly like sex,
you thought of nothing else if you didn't have it
and thought of other things if you did.*

—James Baldwin

❧

Ready money is Aladdin's lamp.

—Lord Byron

*M*oney *is like manure.*
It does best when it is spread around.

—Thomas Fuller, M.D.

*H*onesty *is the best policy—when there is money in it.*

—Mark Twain

*L*ack *of money is no obstacle.*
Lack of an idea is an obstacle.

—Ken Hakuta

14

MATH AND SCIENCE

*Wonder, rather than doubt,
is the root of knowledge.*

—*Abraham Joshua Heschel*

*Scientists are curious athletes, as science is
systemized inquiry followed by a leap of imagination.*

—Noah benShea

❧

*That is the essence of science: ask an impertinent question,
and you are on your way to a pertinent answer.*

—Jacob Bronowski

❧

*The greatest tragedy of science—the slaying of
a beautiful hypothesis by an ugly fact.*

—Thomas Henry Huxley

❧

*I am sorry to say that there is too much point
to the wisecrack that life is extinct on other planets
because their scientists were more advanced than ours.*

—John F. Kennedy

❧

*Science at best is not wisdom; it is knowledge.
Wisdom is knowledge tempered with judgement.*

—Lord Ritchie-Calder

❧

*It is a good morning exercise for a research scientist to discard
a pet hypothesis every day before breakfast. It keeps him young.*

—Konrad Lorenz

*Man has wrestled from nature the power
to make the world a desert or to make the deserts bloom.
There is no evil in the atom; only in men's souls.*

—Adlai E. Stevenson

❧

True science teaches, above all, to doubt and to be ignorant.

—Miguel De Unamuno

❧

If a man's wit be wandering, let him study the mathematics.

—Francis Bacon

❧

*One has to be able to count if only so that at fifty
one doesn't marry a girl of twenty.*

—Maxim Gorky

❧

*Mathematics may be defined as the subject in which
we never know what we are talking about,
nor whether what we are saying is true.*

—Bertrand Russell

❧

*A man has one hundred dollars and you leave him
with two dollars, that's subtraction.*

—Mae West

One aim of the physical sciences has been to give an exact picture of the material world. One achievement of physics in the twentieth century has been to prove that that aim is unattainable.

—Jacob Bronowski

In place of science, the Eskimo has only magic to bridge the gap between what he can understand and what is not known. Without magic, his life would be one long panic.

—Peter Farb

The means by which we live have outdistanced the ends for which we live. Our scientific power has outrun our spiritual power. We have guided missiles and misguided men.

—Martin Luther King, Jr.

In science, all facts, no matter how trivial or banal, enjoy democratic equality.

—Mary McCarthy

It is not merely the truth of science that makes it beautiful, but its simplicity.

—Walker Percy

The simplest schoolboy is now familiar with truths for which Archimedes would have sacrificed his life.

—Ernest Renan

In art nothing worth doing can be done without genius;
in science even a very moderate capacity
can contribute to a supreme achievement.

—Bertrand Russell

❧

Science, by itself, cannot supply us with an ethic.
It can show us how to achieve a given end, and
it may show us that some ends cannot be achieved.

—Bertrand Russell

❧

The true scientist never loses the faculty of amazement.
It is the essence of his being.

—Hans Selye

❧

The power of thinking has two servants:
the power of memory and the power of imagination.

—Zohar

❧

The essential is not to find but to investigate and pursue it.

—Max Nordau

❧

Coincidence is God's way of remaining anonymous.

—Albert Einstein

*Science when well digested is nothing
but good sense and reason.*
—Stanislaus I of Poland

*Science is the most intimate school
of resignation and humility, for it teaches us how
to bow before the seemingly most insignificant of facts.*
—Miguel De Unamuno

Arithmetic is a certain and infallible Art.
—Thomas Hobbes

Heavier-than-air flying machines are impossible.
—Lord Kelvin (President of
the Royal Society in 1895)

*I think there is a world market
for maybe 5 computers.*
—Thomas Watson
(Chairman of IBM in 1943)

640K of computer memory ought to be enough for anybody.
—Bill Gates in 1981

The future ain't what it used to be.
—Yogi Berra

*Science is the great antidote to the
poison of enthusiasm and superstition.*

—Adam Smith

The sciences are pearls strung on a cord of faith.

—Joshua Steinberg

Reality will always remain unknowable.

—Sigmund Freud

*A theory can be proved by experiment; but
no path leads from experiment to birth of a theory.*

—Albert Einstein

Scientists are Peeping Toms at the keyhole of eternity.

—Arthur Koestler

*Life is not always wonderful
but it is an experience filled with wonder.*

—Noah benShea

15

PERSONNEL AND PROGRAM EVALUATION

All of our final decisions are made in states of mind that do not last.

—Marcel Proust

*There is much worth doing and much gained
from looking at what we have done.*

—Noah benShea

❧

*Learning from experience, learning from people,
learning from success and failures, learning
from leaders and followers: personality is formed
in these reactions to stimuli in social environments.*

—James MacGregor Burns

❧

*The ultimate test of practical leadership
is the realization of intended, real change
that meets people's enduring needs.*

—James MacGregor Burns

❧

They that govern must make the least noise.

—John Selden

❧

A staff can be no better than the man it serves.

—David Halberstam

❧

Set the saddle on the right horse.

—John Clarke

If one person calls you an ass, think about it.
If a second person calls you an ass, think about it some more.
If a third person call you an ass, think about putting on a saddle.
—Yiddish proverb

Always mistrust a subordinate
who never finds fault with his superior.
—John Churtin Collins

The more you establish parameters and encourage people to
take initiatives within those boundaries, the more you multiply
your own effectiveness by the effectiveness of other people.
—Robert Hass

Get in a lot of youngsters who don't know it can't be done.
—William Randolph Hearst

The art of choosing men is not nearly so difficult as the art
of enabling those one has chosen to attain their full worth.
—Napoleon

A man in power must have men around him
whom his awesome power does not intimidate.
—William Safire

Tasks must be delegated
without responsibilities being abdicated.

—Anonymous

❦

When a person points a finger at someone else, they should
remember that three of their fingers are pointing at themselves.

—Anonymous

❦

No sooner do we think we have assembled a comfortable life
than we find a piece of ourselves that has no place to fit in.

—Gail Sheehey

❦

Life is a rat-race and the rats are winning.

—Lily Tomlin

❦

Maturity is the ability to do a job whether or not you are
supervised, to carry money without spending it and
to bear an injustice without wanting to get even.

—Ann Landers

❦

Nothing great was ever achieved without enthusiasm.

—Ralph Waldo Emerson

*Against every great and noble idea
are a thousand mediocre minds.*

—Albert Einstein

He that would be a leader must be a bridge.

—Welsh proverb

*Never tell people how to do things. Tell them what to do
and they will surprise you with their ingenuity.*

—General George S. Patton, Jr.

Sometimes the fool that rushes in gets the job done.

—Al Bernstein

High expectations are the key to everything.

—Sam Walton

*Most of us don't ask for what we want
and appear surprised when we don't get it.*

—Noah benShea

There are no menial jobs, only menial attitudes.

—William J. Bennett

If you have a job without any aggravations,
you don't have a job.

—Malcolm S. Forbes

❧

Do not seek to follow in the footsteps of the men of old;
seek what they sought.

—Basho

❧

Always remember that the soundest way to progress in any
organization is to help the man ahead of you to get promoted.

—L. S. Hamaker

❧

There is no greater delight than to be conscious
of sincerity on self-examination.

—Mencius

❧

He who hesitates is sometimes saved.

—James Thurber

❧

All progress has resulted from
people who took unpopular positions.

—Adlai E. Stevenson

*M*en can starve from lack of self-realization
as much as they can from a lack of bread.
—Richard Wright

*J*udgment comes from experience, and
great judgment comes from bad experience.
—American proverb

*T*here is always a latent tension
between what facilitates timely decision and
what promotes thoroughness and accuracy in assessment.
—Richard K. Betts

*F*ew great men could pass Personnel.
—Paul Goodman

*I*n any decision situation, the amount of
relevant information available is inversely proportional
to the importance of the decision.
—Cooke's law

*I*f we are fortunate we love our work.
If we are wise we will work at love.
—Noah benShea

Progress never marches in a parade.

                         —Walter Winchell

What happens to a man is less significant than what happens within him.

                         —Louis L. Mann

16

PROFESSIONAL DEVELOPMENT

Men stumble over the truth from time to time but most pick themselves up and hurry off as if nothing happened.

—Winston Churchill

We often complain that someone isn't the person they once were when the real question is if we're ready to accept them for the person they might yet become.

—Noah benShea

❧

You never will be the person you can be if pressure, tension and discipline are taken out of your life.

—James G. Billay

❧

To be what we are, and to become what we are capable of becoming, is the only end of life.

—Baruch Spinoza

❧

You must live in the present, launch yourself on every wave, find your eternity in each moment.

—Henry David Thoreau

❧

I am still learning.

—Michelangelo

❧

The most rewarding things you do in life are often the ones that look like they cannot be done.

—Arnold Palmer

The relationships we have with the world are largely
determined by the relationship we have with ourselves.

—Greg Anderson

❧

Private victories precede public victories. You can't invert that
process any more than you can harvest a crop before you plant it.

—Stephen Covey

❧

Private deceits inevitably lead to public deceits.

—Noah benShea

❧

One of the greatest moments in anybody's developing experience
is when he no longer tries to hide from himself but
determines to get acquainted with himself as he really is.

—Norman Vincent Peale

❧

By stretching yourself beyond your perceived level
of confidence you accelerate your development of competence.

—Michael Gelb and Tony Buzan

❧

Don't water your weeds.

—Harvey Mackay

Happiness and misery depend not on how high up or low down you are—they depend not upon these, but on the direction in which you are tending.

—Samuel Butler

❧

If you want to increase your success rate, double your failure rate.

—Thomas Watson

❧

All change is a miracle to contemplate, but it is a miracle which is taking place every instant.

—Henry David Thoreau

❧

A miracle is our ability to see the common in an uncommon way.

—Noah benShea

❧

Nurture your mind with great thoughts. To believe in the heroic makes heroes.

—Benjamin Disraeli

❧

A smooth sea never made a skilled mariner.

—English proverb

Self-development is a higher duty than self-sacrifice.
—Elizabeth Cady Stanton

To be thrown upon one's own resources, is to be cast into the very lap of fortune; for our faculties then undergo a development and display an energy of which they were previously unsusceptible.
—Ben Franklin

Inside yourself or outside, you never have to change what you see, only the way you see it.
—Thaddeus Golas

Live to learn and you will learn to live.
—Portuguese proverb

Before a diamond shows its brilliancy and prismatic colors it has to stand a good deal of cutting and smoothing.
—Anonymous

If you think you're nothing special and feel like you're under a lot of pressure, remember that an ordinary chunk of coal under tremendous pressure for a long time becomes a diamond.
—Noah benShea

*The gem cannot be polished without friction,
nor a man perfected without trials.*

—Chinese proverb

∽

*Create the kind of climate in your organization where
personal growth is expected, recognized, and rewarded.*

—Anonymous

∽

We grow because we struggle, we learn and overcome.

—R. C. Allen

∽

*If you wag your tail when someone brings out your leash,
think about it.*

—Noah benShea

∽

*The Chinese word for "crisis" is made up from two other
characters. One is danger. And the other is opportunity.*

—Noah benShea

∽

*In studying the history of the human mind one is impressed
again and again by the fact that the growth of the mind is the
widening of the range of consciousness, and that each step forward
has been a most painful and laborious achievement.*

—Carl Jung

17

READING, WRITING, AND LANGUAGE ARTS

Education is what you get from reading the fine print. Experience is what you get from not reading it.

—Anonymous

Many people read, but it is the wise who can read themselves.
—Noah benShea

Fill your paper with the breathings of your heart.
—William Wordsworth

*Thought is the blossom; language the bud;
action the fruit behind it.*
—Ralph Waldo Emerson

*The quality of our thoughts is bordered on all sides
by our facility with language.*
—J. Michael Straczynski

*To me, the greatest pleasure of writing is not what it's about,
but the music the words make.*
—Truman Capote

It is the silence between the notes that makes the music.
—Noah benShea

*Literature is the art of writing something
that will be read twice.*
—Cyril Connolley

I learned that you should feel when writing,
not like Lord Byron on a mountain top, but like child
stringing beads in kindergarten—happy, absorbed,
and quietly putting one bead on after another.

—Brenda Ueland

*N*o nation ancient or modern ever lost the liberty
of freely speaking, writing, or publishing their sentiments,
but forthwith lost their liberty in general and became slaves.

—John Peter Zenger

*W*e live at the level of our language. Whatever we can articulate
we can imagine or explore. All you have to do to educate a child—
leave him alone and teach him to read. The rest is brainwashing.

—Ellen Gilcrist

*Y*ou don't have to burn books to destroy a culture.
Just get people to stop reading them.

—Ray Bradbury

*R*eading is to the mind what exercise is to the body.

—Sir Richard Steele

*W*hat we call education and culture is for the most part
nothing but the substitution of reading for experience, of literature
for life, of the obsolete fictitious for the contemporary real.

—George Bernard Shaw

No race can prosper till it learns that there is as much dignity in tilling a field as in writing a poem.

—Booker T. Washington

How many a man has dated a new era in his life from the reading of a book?

—Henry David Thoreau

Learn as much by writing as by reading.

—Lord Acton

Reading makes a full man, conference a ready man, and writing an exact man.

—Francis Bacon

Resolve to edge in a little reading every day, if it is but a single sentence. If you gain fifteen minutes a day, it will make itself felt at the end of the year.

—Horace Mann

Reading furnishes the mind only with materials of knowledge, it is thinking that makes what we read ours.

—John Locke

The pleasure of all reading is doubled when one lives with another who shares the same books.

—Katherine Mansfield

Happy is he who has laid up in his youth, and held fast in all future, a genuine and passionate love of reading.

—Rufus Choate

It is well to read everything of something and something of everything.

—Henry Peter Brougham

The reading of all good books is like conversations with the finest men of past centuries.

—Descartes

Some books are undeservedly forgotten; none are undeservedly remembered.

—W. H. Auden

Books give not wisdom where there was none before But where some is, reading makes it more.

—Sir John Harrington

Writing comes more easily if you have something to say.

—Sholem Asch

If you would be a reader, read; if you would be a writer, write.

—Epictetus

18

RESEARCH AND ACCOUNTABILITY

What is research, but a blind date with knowledge.

—Will Henry

*D*o what you say and say what you have done.

—*Noah benShea*

༄

*E*very private citizen has a public responsibility.

—*Myra Janco Daniels*

༄

*W*hen you take stuff from one writer, it's plagiarism;
but when you take it from many writers it's research.

—*Wilson Mizner*

༄

*Y*ou can't run a society or cope with its problems if people
are not held accountable for what they do.

—*John Leo*

༄

A human being's first responsibility is
to shake hands with him- or herself.

—*Henry Winkler*

༄

*D*eceiving somebody for his own good is a responsibility that
should be shouldered only by the gods.

—*Henry S. Haskins*

༄

*G*ive a man a mask, and he will tell you the truth.

—*Oscar Wilde*

Few things help an individual more than to place responsibility upon him and to let him know that you trust him.

—Booker T. Washington

If you want your children to keep their feet on the ground, put some responsibility on their shoulders.

—Abigail Van Buren

*Dignity doesn't come with the job.
Dignity is what we bring to our work.*

—Noah benShea

*Rank does not confer privilege or give power.
It imposes responsibility.*

—Peter Drucker

*Education is more than a luxury;
it is a responsibility that society owes to itself.*

—Robin Cook

*It is better to do your own duty, however imperfectly,
than to assume the duties of another person.*

—Bhagavad Gita

The reward of one duty is the power to fulfill another.

—George Eliot

To live without duties is obscene.

—Ralph Waldo Emerson

This is your duty, to act well the part that is given to you.

—Epictetus

*The still small voice within you must always be the final
arbiter when there is a conflict of duty.*

—Mohandas K. Gandhi

*A succession of small duties always faithfully done
demands no less than do heroic actions.*

—Jean-Jacques Rousseau

Pursue the nearest duty.

—Friedrich von Schiller

*If politics is the art of the possible,
research is surely the art of the solvable.*

—Sir Peter Medawar

*I believe that every right implies a responsibility;
every opportunity, an obligation; every possession, a duty.*

—John D. Rockefeller

The buck stops here.

—Harry S. Truman

Our privileges can be no greater than our obligations.
The protection of our rights can endure no longer
than the performance of our responsibilities.

—John F. Kennedy

I leave this rule for others when I'm dead:
Be always sure you're right—then go ahead.

—David Crockett

Re-search, by definition, means to look and look again.
And who among us would not see more for
taking a second look? And a third.

—Noah benShea

The reward of a thing well done, is to have done it.

—Ralph Waldo Emerson

19

SCHOOL CHANGE

A permanent state of transition is man's most noble condition.

—Juan Ramon Jimenez

Change is the only constant.

—Noah benShea

≈

My grandmother wanted me to have an education,
so she kept me out of school.

—Margaret Mead

≈

No man puts his foot in the same river twice.
Not the same river. Not the same man.

—Heraclitus

≈

What is actual is actual only for a time.
And only for one place.

—T. S. Eliot

≈

Every season they change the clothing on the mannequins
but underneath the dummies remain the same.

—Noah benShea

≈

When you get there, there isn't any there there.

—Gertrude Stein

≈

Every new adjustment is a crisis in self-esteem.

—Eric Hoffer

The classic definition of neurotic behavior is when we choose what is negative but familiar over what is positive but new.

—*Noah benShea*

Turbulence is life force.

—*Ramsey Clark*

A capacity to change is indispensable. Equally indispensable is the capacity to hold fast to that which is good.

—*John Foster Dulles*

To everything there is a season.

—*Ecclesiastes*

Feelings are seasons. Seasons change.

—*Noah benShea*

The law of life, so cruel and so just, demands that one must grow or else pay more for remaining the same.

—*Norman Mailer*

Everything and everyone continues in its state of rest, or of uniform motion, unless it is compelled to change that state by forces impressed upon it.

—*Sir Isaac Newton*

*Nothing is unchangeable but the inherent
and inalienable rights of man.*

—Thomas Jefferson

Can the Ethiopian change his skin, or the leopard his spots?

—Jeremiah

What does not bend, breaks.

—Noah benShea

*We started from scratch, every American an immigrant who
came because he wanted a change.*

—Eleanor Roosevelt

Change is not progress.

—H. L. Mencken

*If people do not grow into who they might yet become,
they grow who into who they were.*

—Noah benShea

*A relationship is like a shark;
unless it is moving forward it dies.*

—Woody Allen

If you want to give God a good laugh, talk of your plans.

—Yiddish proverb

Progress always involves risks. You can't steal second base and keep your foot on first.

—Fredrick B. Wilcox

Before we try to change the world maybe we should try to improve our neighborhood.

—Noah benShea

First I saw the mountains were mountains and the rivers were rivers. Then I saw that mountains were not mountains and rivers were not rivers. And then I saw that mountains were mountains and rivers were rivers.

—Taoist teaching

20
SCHOOL
SAFETY

Most people want security in
this world, not liberty.

—H. L. Mencken

Our mind is less limited by our intellect than by our fears and insecurities. Our fears frame our future.

—Noah benShea

In skating over thin ice, our safety is in our speed.

—Ralph Waldo Emerson

A ship in harbor is safe—but that is not what ships are for.

—John A. Shedd

We spend out time searching for security and hate it when we get it.

—John Steinbeck

A mind that does not feel safe will never step out of its ignorance.

—Noah benShea

The less secure a man is, the more likely he is to have extreme prejudices.

—Clint Eastwood

Close scrutiny will show that most "crisis situations" are opportunities to either advance, or stay where you are.

—Dr. Maxwell Maltz

*If you're so sure of what you think,
why do I have to agree with you?*

—Noah benShea

෨

*For happiness one needs security, but joy can spring like a
flower even from the cliffs of despair.*

—Anne Morrow Lindbergh

෨

Fasten your seat belts. It's going to be a bumpy night.

—Joseph L. Mankiewicz

෨

Things don't have to be good for us to be great.

—Noah benShea

෨

*Walk down the path in life and be prepared for the most awful
thing to jump out and attack you. Walk down the path in life
and be prepared for the most wonderful thing to jump out and
embrace you. Walk down the path in life and be prepared for
nothing to happen at all. Walk down the path in life and be
prepared for all three events to happen concurrently.*

—Zen truth

෨

*If the highest aim of a captain were to preserve his ship,
he would keep it in port forever.*

—St. Thomas Aquinas

*D*istrust and caution are the parents of security.
—Benjamin Franklin

*H*e that is too secure is not safe.
—Thomas Fuller

*L*iberty is in fact only a secondary need;
the primary need is security.
—Bertrand de Jouvenel

*O*nly in growth, reform, and change, paradoxically enough,
is true security to be found.
—Anne Morrow Lindbergh

*T*hey that can give up essential liberty to obtain a
little temporary safety deserve neither liberty nor safety.
—Benjamin Franklin

I respect faith, but doubt is what gets you an education.
—Wilson Mizner

*A*nxiety is the reaction to danger.
—Sigmund Freud

Neurotic anxiety is the fear of fear.

—Noah benShea

❧

Forewarned is forearmed.

—Cervantes

❧

*Those who prepared for all the emergencies of life beforehand
may equip themselves at the expense of joy.*

—E. M. Foster

❧

*Where observation is concerned,
chance favors only the prepared mind.*

—Louis Pasteur

❧

If you want a guarantee in life, buy a vacuum cleaner.

—Noah benShea

❧

*We cannot make it rain, but we can see to it that
the rain falls on prepared soil.*

—Henri J. M. Nouwen

❧

No tears. No rainbows.

—Noah benShea

Hope for the best and prepare for the worst.
—English saying

∽

Hope for the best and make peace with the rest.
—Noah benShea

∽

Trust in Allah but tie your camel.
—Middle Eastern proverb

∽

Security is mostly superstition.
—Helen Keller

21

TEACHER PREPARATION

*The secret to getting ahead
is getting started.*

—Mark Twain

*T*oo often we are ready, fire, aim and
wonder why we miss our target.

—Noah benShea

*G*ood teaching is one fourth preparation
and three fourths theatre.

—Gail Godwin

*T*he butterfly becomes a butterfly
only when it's entirely ready.

—Chinese proverb

*T*he best preparation for good work tomorrow
is good work today.

—Elbert Hubbard

*T*he best way to prepare for life is to begin to live.

—Elbert Hubbard

*F*our steps to achievement: Plan purposefully, prepare
prayerfully, proceed positively, pursue persistently.

—William A. Ward

Chance favors the prepared mind.

—Louis Pasteur

He who is well prepared has half won the battle.

—Portuguese proverb

Failures don't plan to fail; they fail to plan.

—Harvey Mackay

The majority of men are bundles of beginnings.

—Ralph Waldo Emerson

We're not lost in a dream. We're only dreaming we're lost.

—Noah benShea

One of these days is none of these days.

—H. G. Bohn

The most pathetic person in the world is someone who has sight, but has no vision.

—Helen Keller

*D*on't wait for your "ship to come in" and feel angry and
cheated when it doesn't. Get going with something small.

—Irene Kassorla

*I*t is always wise to look ahead, but difficult
to look farther than you can see.

—Winston Churchill

*W*e are people with lanterns going in search of the light.

—Noah benShea

*D*on't agonize. Organize.

—Florynce Kennedy

*S*top the habit of wishful thinking and
start the habit of thoughtful wishes.

—Mary Martin

*T*o have ideas is to gather flowers;
to think is to weave them into garlands.

—Anne Sophie Swetchire

*D*ecide what you want, decide what you are willing to
exchange for it. Establish your priorities and go to work.

—H. L. Hunt

The most important thing in business is sincerity.
If you can fake that you have it made.
                                        —Groucho Marx.

                        ☙

A thought that does not result in action is nothing much.
And an action that does not proceed
from a thought is nothing at all.
                                        —Georges Bernanos

                        ☙

Wisely and slow; they stumble that run fast.
                                        —William Shakespeare

                        ☙

When you are in a hurry, go slowly.
                                        —Japanese proverb

                        ☙

Haste manages all things badly.
                                        —Publius Papinius Statius

                        ☙

Sometimes what a man escapes to is worse
than what he escapes from.
                                        —Stan Lyne

*W*ho begins much, finishes little.

—German proverb

*Y*ou can't hatch chickens from fried eggs.

—Pennsylvania Dutch
proverb

A rock pile ceases to be a rock pile the moment
a single person contemplates it, bearing within himself
the image of a cathedral.

—Antoine de Saint-Exupery

TECHNOLOGY

The world is so fast that there are days when the person who says it can't be done is interrupted by the person who is doing it.

—Anonymous

To get where you are going begins with
being where you are now.

—Noah benShea

❧

It is only when they go wrong that machines
remind you how powerful they are.

—Clive James

❧

Man is a tool-making animal.

—Benjamin Franklin

❧

If I had to choose, I would rather have birds than airplanes.

—Charles Lindbergh

❧

Ours is a world of nuclear giants and ethical infants. If we
continue to develop our technology without wisdom or prudence,
our servant may prove to be our executioner.

—General Omar N. Bradley

❧

I know not with what weapons World War Three will be
fought, but World War Four will be fought with sticks and stones.

—Albert Einstein

*Technological progress is like an axe in
the hands of a pathological criminal.*

—Albert Einstein

❧

The medium is the message.

—Marshall McLuhan

❧

*We live in a society exquisitely dependent on science and
technology, in which hardly anyone knows anything
about science and technology.*

—Carl Sagan

❧

Progress would be wonderful—if only it would stop.

—Robert Musil

❧

*Our progress as a nation can be no swifter
than our progress in education.*

—John F. Kennedy

❧

*There are many ways of going forward,
but only one way of standing still.*

—Franklin D. Roosevelt

Science and technology multiply around us. To an increasing extent they dictate the languages in which we speak and think. Either we use those languages, or we remain mute.

—J. G. Ballard

⌒

However far modern science and techniques have fallen short of their inherent possibilities, they have taught mankind at least one lesson: Nothing is impossible.

—Lewis Mumford

⌒

The most important function of art and science is to awaken the cosmic religious feeling and keep it alive.

—Albert Einstein

⌒

Our Age of Anxiety is, in great part, the result of trying to do today's job with yesterday's tools.

—Marshall McLuhan

⌒

The only way to discover the limits of the possible is to go beyond them into the impossible.

—Arthur Clarke

⌒

Any sufficiently advanced technology is indistinguishable from magic.

—Arthur Clarke

Technology is dominated by two types of people: those who understand what they do not manage, and those who manage what they do not understand.

—Putt's Law

❧

For a list of all the ways technology has failed to improve the quality of life, please press three.

—Alice Kahn

❧

Technology makes it possible for people to gain control over everything, except over technology.

—John Tudor

❧

All technology should be assumed guilty until proven innocent.

—David Brower

❧

Technological progress has merely provided us with more efficient means for going backwards.

—Aldous Huxley

❧

All process is not necessarily progress.
All progress is not necessarily painless.

—Noah benShea

23

WOMEN IN EDUCATION

If you educate a man you educate a person, but if you educate a woman you educate a family.

—Ruby Manikan

Our roles in life change. Time is the great casting director.

            —Noah benShea

When women take on a career, they don't discard their female values, but add them on to the traditional male values of work achievement and career success.

            —Susan Sturdinent
            and Gail Donoff

Women know a lot of things and nobody can figure out how they know them.

            —Maridel Le Sueur

Women's work is always toward wholeness.

            —May Sarton

Whatever women do they must do it twice as well as men to be thought half as good. Luckily this is not difficult.

            —Charlotte Whitton

Anyone who knows anything of history knows that great social changes are impossible without feminine upheaval.

            —Karl Marx

There is a woman at the beginning of all great things.
—Alphonse de Lamartine

❧

The emotional, sexual, and psychological stereotyping of females begins with the doctor saying "It's a girl."
—Shirley Chisholm

❧

Beware the fury of a patient woman.
—Anonymous

❧

Life is a negotiation.
—Wendy Wasserstein

❧

Female passion is to masculine as an epic is to an epigram.
—Karl Kraus

❧

If you want something said, ask a man.
If you want something done, ask a woman.
—Margaret Thatcher

❧

Because I am a woman, I must make unusual efforts to succeed. If I fail, no one will say "She doesn't have what it takes," they will say "Women don't have what it takes."
—Clare Boothe Luce

A happy woman is one who has no cares at all, a cheerful woman is one who has cares but doesn't let them get her down.

—Beverly Sills

❧

*F*or every woman who makes a fool out of a man there is another woman who makes a man out of a fool.

—Samuel Hoffman

❧

*W*omen are like tea bags; put them in hot water and they get stronger.

—Eleanor Roosevelt

❧

*F*or my part I distrust all generalizations about women, favorable and unfavorable, masculine and feminine, ancient and modern; all alike, I should say, result from paucity of experience.

—Bertrand Russell

❧

*S*he opens her mouth with wisdom.

—Book of Proverbs

❧

*D*o not call for black power or green power. Call for brain power.

—Barbara Jordan

CORWIN
PRESS

The Corwin Press logo—a raven striding across an open book—represents the happy union of courage and learning. We are a professional-level publisher of books and journals for K–12 educators, and we are committed to creating and providing resources that embody these qualities. Corwin's motto is "Success for All Learners."